DEVELOPING GODLY CHARACTER FOR A HIGHER ALTITUDE

HEALTHY CHURCH BIBLE STUDY SERIES
Volume One

BY

ADEBAYO S. DAVID

Cornerstone Publishing

A Division of Cornerstone Creativity Group LLC
Phone: +1(516) 547-4999
info@thecornerstonepublishers.com
www.thecornerstonepublishers.com

To order bulk copies of this book or to contact the author please email: greaterthingsnow@yahoo.com

CONTENTS

INTRODUCTION

The HEALTHY CHURCH SERIES is a series of Bible study teachings developed to encourage pastors to build a healthy church environment, based on the word of God, where believers can grow, learn and thrive spiritually, mentally, maritally and financially in life and in the kingdom of God. This is in with Paul's admonition in

1 Timothy 3:15 to teach people how to behave in the house of God, which is the church of the living God, "THE PILLAR AND GROUND OF TRUTH".

This book is designed to ensure godly characters and attitudes in believers that can make them succeed anywhere and in all aspects of life – personal Christian walk, marriage, ministry, business, academics and relationships of any kind - knowing full well the word of God and the mind of God concerning any subject that affects their lives in Christ.

Nations and people that prosper are people who have built their lives on the "truth of life" - which is Jesus Christ. He said, "You shall know the truth and the truth shall set you free. Only the truth that you know and the truth that is revealed to you can set you free!

TIME OF REFRESHING AND SEASON OF REVIVAL

TEXT: ACTS 3:19; HABAKKUK 3:2

If there is any time that we need to cry for revival, it is now. The need for revival today in our lives, communities, churches and nation is much more paramount now than ever before.

If Prophet Habakkuk could cry in his day, when things were still relatively better, when moral values were cherished, and personal discipline and the fear of God were of utmost importance, then we should be doing even much more today. Oh, how much we need revival in these days of moral decadence, rampant perversions, family dysfunctions, political upheavals, economic downturn, ravaging diseases, as well as widespread backsliding, heresies, worldliness, and mixed multitude in the church!

In the early days of the church, the power of God and his Spirit were so present and mighty, so much that people developed such a great reverence for the things of God (Acts 5:11). But, alas, the case is different today. It has become so difficult to differentiate a believer from a non-believer. The church is so joined to the world that we sometimes cannot differentiate between both. Oh, how we need a new season of revival and time of refreshing!

Why is it that we do not often experience the awesome power of God, as the early believers did? It is because iniquities abound in the church today. The sons of Zion (the church) that were once likened to fine gold, have become dim and the stones of the sanctuary have become scattered! (Lamentations 4:1-2).

We certainly need the mercy of God. We need a new season of revival so that the time of refreshing can come from God to us.

SIGNS THAT YOU NEED A TRUE REVIVAL

1. Poor spiritual attitude (Revelation 3:15-19). When you have become lukewarm or indifferent to the things of God. When there is no passion in your service, prayer life and commitment.

2. Reduced love for God and the things of God (Revelation 2:1-5). Do you now prefer to watch home videos or engaging in other amusing indulgences than to watch sermons or participate in other spiritual activities?

3. Neglect of Bible reading (Acts 6:2).

4. Neglect of prayer - personal and corporate (Jeremiah 5:1, 23-25).

5. Indifference towards the souls of the unsaved (Matthew 12:11-12:7).

6. Ingratitude. When've become unthankful to God and men. (2 Timothy 3:2).

7. Hypocritical living – that is, living a double life (Job 15: 34).

8. Neglect of family time, family devotion and personal quiet time.

9. Neglect to watch over fellow believers.

10. Inability to live in self-denial - no more fasting, vigils or any other activity that inconveniences the flesh.

11. Worldly-mindedness and excessive attachment to earthly things (Colossians 3:1-2).

12. Manifesting a critical spirit.

13. Manifesting a proud or lustful spirit.

14. Manifesting a manipulative spirit.

15. Manifesting bad temper.

16. Robbing God of tithes and offering.

17. Hindering others from being useful in God's vineyard.

18. Loss of passion for soul-winning.

19. Unwillingness to identify as a Christian.

20. Feeling ashamed to hold or read your Bible during break at work or in a public place.

21. Getting irritated by your spouse/parent or children's commitment to prayer or other spiritual activities.

HOW TO START A SEASON OF REVIVAL

The following are required for a true revival:

1. Sincere Repentance (Acts 3:19)

Every true revival is always preceded by a fervent conviction of sin and followed by an intense desire to live in obedience to God. It involves giving up one's will to God in deep humility and repentance. Repentance is **turning away from** sin, not just confessing and continuing in it.

Apostle Peter told the teeming crowd of the Jews watching the arrival and move of the Holy Spirit upon the early believers, "If you want to see the power of and glory of God, it is time for sincere repentance." Essentially, therefore, repentance comes before revival.

Asking for a revival without a conscious and resolute willingness to repent from sin, is like putting the cart before the horse and expecting a smooth ride. There must first be a preparation of the heart, the softening of the hardness of the heart, before God will give true revival. Otherwise, the most we will see will be the mist or dew of revival, and not the true showers that brings real refreshing.

2. Preparation of the Heart (Hosea 10:12; Proverbs 16:1-2).

Hosea 10:12 reads, "**Sow for yourselves righteousness; Reap in mercy; Break up your fallow ground, For it is time to seek the LORD, Till He comes and rains righteousness on you.**"

Revival is the raining down of righteousness by God upon us, His people. Righteousness is the ability to be in right standing with God and before God. This cannot be achieved without the preparation of the heart; that is, the removal of weeds from the ground of our heart.

There is no true farmer that plants on an uncultivated and untilled land. Our heart is like a ground or farmland, upon which the weeds and thorns of life tend to grow, and consequently hindering the blessing of revival. This kind of uncultivated ground receive nothing but a curse. Hebrew 6:7-8 says, "**For the earth which drinks in the rain that often comes upon it, and bears herbs useful for those by whom it is cultivated, receives**

9

blessing from God; but if it bears thorns and briers, it is rejected and near to being cursed, whose end is to be burned."

3. Softening of the Heart (Hosea 10:12)

If you must break up the fallow ground of your heart, you must begin by looking at yourself. Examine and know the state of your heart. Ask sincere questions from yourself and give yourself sincere answers. Ask the following questions:

- Am I still in the faith? (2 Corinthians 13:5)

- Do I still love God like I used to, when I first gave my life to Him? What is my devotion like, in terms of prayer, Bible study, and fellowship with the saints?

- Do I still wholeheartedly do the things of God that have always mattered to me?

- How much of my flesh has been conquered?

- Am I filled with inordinate craving or pride over flashy cars, houses and worldly riches to the detriment of my spiritual growth and pursuit of eternity? (Mark 4:18-19)

- Do I not love this world and the things of this world more than God? And would I not even compromise to have the things of this world at the expense of my eternity? (1 John 2:15-17)

10

If you have clearly examined yourself and found yourself wanting in any of the above areas, then it is time to seek God genuinely in prayer, to break the fallow ground of your heart, so that the rain of revival can be released upon you and there will be a time of refreshing and renewal of mercy upon your life.

Self-examination is looking into your life to assess your true standing before God. It is a comparative evaluation of your present life with the way you were when you newly began your Christian life, to see whether you are making progress or slowing down or even backslidden.

Indeed, if we must experience a season of revival and time of refreshing, we must take a critical look at the state of our lives and not just glance through. We will need the searchlights of the Holy Spirit and the Word of God to reveal where we stand. In doing so, we must go to God and make true confessions, where necessary. Thereafter, we will need to ask for grace not to return to any of our transgressions again.

IT IS TIME TO TURN TO GOD

Psalm 85:4-7; 2 Chronicles 7:14

When we turn to God with a true heart-rending and soul-searching revival prayer, like the psalmist in Psalms 51 and 85, God will hear us and revive us again and there will be seasons of revival and times of refreshing.

CONCLUSION

It is time to seek the lord with the whole of our heart

PRAYER

1. Oh Lord, search me through and through (Psalm 139:23-24).

2. Oh Lord, break me and remold me (Hosea 10:12).

3. Oh Lord, revive my spirit, soul and body (Psalm 85:6; Habakkuk 3:2).

NOTES

NOTES

_____

_____

_____

_____

_____

_____

_____

_____

_____

_____

STUDY 2

REVIVAL PRAYING

TEXT: ISAIAH 64:5

Revival praying is a worthwhile engagement that has the power to bring great transformation to our individual lives, families, churches and communities. However, before we fully delve into what revival praying is all about, we need to look into what prayer itself is.

A lot of us have wrong notions about prayer. We assume prayer to be what it is not. Many believe that prayer is merely talking to God. Some believe that prayer is asking and receiving. Some believe that prayer is sending God on an errand to help us kill our enemies and collect our stolen blessings. While others believe it is asking God to help us deal with people we don't like or perceive as our enemies.

The truth however is that prayer is much more than merely getting God to run an errand for us. And it is totally different from a beggar knocking at a rich man's door. The word "prayer" actually means "a wish directed towards God." Therefore, true prayer seeks God Himself, for with Him, we get all we need.

Prayer is simply the turning of ourselves to God. King David called it the lifting up of the soul to God (Psalm 25:1). When we lift up our soul to God, it gives Him the opportunity to do what He wills in us and with us.

A Jewish Rabbi said that, "prayer is the moment when heaven and earth kiss each other." God is in the heaven, man is the earth. When man's "natural" comes into conjugation with the "super" of God through prayer, the "supernatural" is released.

WHAT REVIVAL PRAYING IS

What then is revival praying? In 2 Chronicles 7:14, God says, **"If My people who are called by My name will humble themselves, and pray and seek My face, and turn from their wicked ways, then I will hear from heaven, and will forgive their sin and heal their land."** From this scripture, we discover that revival praying is:

1. Humbling ourselves before God. It is a moment of coming down from our high horses - our emotional, psychological, educational and societal high towers of pride, rooted in nothing but self and the flesh. It is stripping ourselves of pride, arrogance and the superfluity of naughtiness (James 1:21). It is killing all filthiness and superficial attachments that are contending with God or have been used to replace God in our lives.

16

2. Seeking the face of God and not his hand alone. The face of God is His likeness, His person, His character, His nature, His purpose, His passion, His desires and His expressions (Psalm 17:15). The hand of God represents His power, His gifts, His blessings and His miracles – all of which a man can have but still perish (Psalm 78:27-31).

3. Turning from our wicked ways, and seeking the power and grace of God to sin no more.

4. Seeking to do what God wants and not persuading God to do what we want Him to do. It is not bending the will of God to ours but bending our will to His. (Psalm 40:7-8).

5. Seeking and thirsting after God - to see His power and to know His way (Psalm 42:1-2).

6. Interceding on behalf of our unsaved loved ones, friends, neighbors, colleagues, church members, fellow citizens and others, until we see them turning back to God (Romans 10:1-4).

7. Seeking to turn lost sinners back to God and reconciling backsliders back to God (and not to ourselves) (2 Corinthians 5:17-18).

8. Repositioning ourselves and the church in fulfilling our God-given assignment on earth – and particularly in the nation where we have been placed - to make positive impacts to the glory of God (Mark16:15-18)

WHAT REVIVAL PRAYING IS NOT

1. It is not the killing of our enemies and sinners. God does not want sinners to perish; He wants all men saved (John 3:16; 2 Peter 3:9).

2. It is not to see power just return to the church, but rather to see the God of power return to His people with power (Malachi 3).

3. It is not to bring the crowd to the church but to bring God to the crowd, who will turn out to be the light of the world (Acts 2:33-41).

4. It is not to see prosperity return to the church. Even though power and prosperity usually accompany every true revival, they are not the primary goals of a revival.

5. It is not a craving for influence over the church or the nation; rather, it is a craving for Christ to influence the actions of His people, who will, in turn, influence their families, communities and the entire nation (Acts11:26; 17:6).

6. It is not bending God's will to our own will, but allowing God to bend our will to His.

7. It is not the propagation of the name of a denomination, a man of God, or group but rather the propagation of the name of Christ.

CONCLUSION

If we are going to experience times of refreshing and seasons of revival, we must earnestly seek God through true intercession and revival praying.

PRAYER

1. Oh Lord, send us true revival by your Spirit.

2. Oh Lord, give us the spirit of intercession.

3. Oh Lord, use me to bring about a true revival of change, power and influence for Christ.

NOTES

_____

_____

_____

_____

_____

_____

_____

_____

_____

_____

NOTES

_____

_____

_____

_____

_____

_____

_____

_____

_____

_____

STUDY 3

INGREDIENTS OF TRUE REVIVAL (PART 1 - BROKENNESS)

TEXT: PSALM 34:18; ISAIAH 51:17; HOSEA10:12

Before there will be an outpouring of the spirit of revival and time of refreshing, the vessels God seeks to pour out His spirit upon must be vessels that are completely broken - broken from the flesh and its works. As Galatians 5:19-21 reveals, the works of the flesh in any individual or congregation are always a barrier to the outpouring to the spirit of revival.

Whenever we are asking for revival, we are actually asking for something very serious, spiritual and never a child's play

Brokenness, the Way of God

The way of God is different from the ways of man. Anything that is broken is deemed by man to be unfit and meant to be cast away. But to God, only that which is broken is useful. Just as flowers yield their perfumes when crushed and grapes produce wine when squashed, so also are the vessels that God uses for revival broken vessels.

God's people are only ready and usable for revival when broken. Revival is the Spirit of Christ that reveals to us our sinfulness, the areas in our lives that need to be broken so that God can do something great with us.

Jacob could not fully experience God's supernatural breakthrough, blessing and grace, until he was broken in the hollow of his thigh (Genesis 32:25-28). It was after this brokenness that God pronounced a trans-generational blessing that brought a lasting impact of revival and the pre-birth of Israel as a nation.

Jacob left that place of prayer limping, but he limped with God's glory, power blessing and revival. Revival, therefore, is contending with God in the place of prayer, until there is a breaking of the hollow of our thigh - which is our flesh – as well as everything else that exacts itself against God and the knowledge of Christ in our lives.

Marks of True Brokenness (Psalm 51: 17)

As we have earlier established, until we are broken, we can neither see God nor experience His power or the outpouring of His Spirit. God only favors and looks upon those who are truly broken in the spirit and upon such He freely grants His Spirit and power (Isaiah 66:2).

The identifiable marks of brokenness that will bring revival are:

1. A broken spirit brings a quickening of conscience and volition.

2. A broken spirit is a sensitive spirit. It discerns what is amiss and does not hurt or grieve the Holy Spirit or fellow believer.

3. A broken spirit is pliable. It is easily entreated, teachable and never reactionary. It is never a closed heart filed with stubbornness.

4. A broken spirit is soft and easily penetrated, while a hard heart cannot be penetrated at all. An unbroken spirit is a type of Nabal spirit; that is, the spirit of foolishness (1 Samuel 25:25).

5. A broken spirit is submissive to God's voice and God's word; it is easily bent to correction.

6. A broken spirit is not conceited or prideful. All ideas of its own importance are gone.

7. A broken spirit has no hypocrisy. It honestly reveals itself to God.

8. A broken spirit has deep sincerity.

9. A prayer from a broken spirit is usually deep and comes from real feelings.

10. A broken spirit does not wait for strong, forceful instructions before obeying.

11. A broken spirit is a surrendered spirit to God's will and ways alone.

12. A broken spirit is conquered by the word of God and does not insist on its own ways.

The Glory of Brokenness

1. When God breaks us, He does so to bring us to Himself.

2. When God breaks us, He reveals Himself through and in us.

3. When God breaks us, His light and presence radiate through us.

4. When God breaks us, power and true spiritual blessings flow through us.

5. When God breaks us, the world comes to the light of Christ shining through us.

6. When God breaks us, self-reputation, personal advertisement and pride are burnt into chaff and blown away from our lives.

7. When God breaks us, there is revival, time of refreshing and showers of blessing.

CONCLUSION

Let us seek the hand of the Potter to break and remold us (Jeremiah 18:1-10).

PRAYER

1. Oh Lord, break me and remold me.

2. Oh Lord, cause everything that has no foundation in Christ that is in me to be uprooted.

3. Oh Lord, break me, mold me, fill me, and use me in Jesus' name.

NOTES

_____

_____

_____

_____

_____

_____

NOTES

STUDY 4

INGREDIENTS OF TRUE REVIVAL (PART 2 - PASSION FOR GOD'S PRESENCE)

TEXT: PSALM 60:1-2; ACTS 3:19

The whole concept of revival is a conscious awakening for the presence of God. As revival sweeps across the land and begins to arouse the hearts of people, God's first call is to bring His people into His presence. This is a call to live our lives, as individuals and as a congregation, in the presence of a living God, being conscious of time of refreshing that He has promised us.

The presence of God is to be the great passion of every believer's heart. We are called to love the presence of the Lord and to desire His presence every day. Note that this is not the presence of any man, pastor, bishop, prophet or apostle but the presence of God Himself.

The pursuit of God's presence supersedes the pursuit of any other thing. When His presence is with us, every other thing will fall in place. When God told Moses in Exodus 33:14, "My Presence will go with you, and I will give you rest", Moses immediately replied, "If Your Presence does not go with us, do not bring us up from here" (verse 15). This shows the power and priority of God's presence in our lives.

Understanding God's Presence (Psalm 68:8)

The presence of God is the conscious awareness of his manifold existence, power, authority and glory in man and around a man (Psalm 114:5-7). A.W. Tozer rightly stated: "God wills that we should push on into His presence and live our whole life there. This is to be known to us in conscious experience. It is more than a doctrine to be held, it is a life to be enjoyed every moment of every day."

Activating God's Presence (Luke 1:19)

There are certain conditions and lifestyle that activate or make manifest the presence of God. First, though, it is important to understand that the presence of God is more than feelings. It is not about goose bumps, shouting, the dramatic or the spectacular. The presence of God is supernatural and cannot be fabricated or birthed in the flesh.

Conditions for Activating God's Presence

1. Being born again by the Spirit of God (John 3: 5-8)

2. Making holiness a daily lifestyle (1 Peter 1:15-16)

3. Commitment to prayer (Acts 4: 31; Colossians 4:2; Romans 12:11)

4. Subjugation of self and the flesh through fasting (Acts 13:2)

5. Living in newness of life by Christ Jesus (Ephesians 4: 1-2)

6. Walking in the Spirit (Galatians 5:16)

7. Walking in love and unity (Ephesians 4:3-6; Psalm 133)

God's Manifest Presence

The manifest presence of God is when God reveals Himself, usually by His own sovereign prerogative. This is the presence of God that can be felt, even when we are not seeking God or practicing the spiritual disciplines of prayer, repentance and other truths that the scripture defines as approaches to the living God. This manifest presence of God is effected by His sovereign power and not through our initiation.

Instances of God's manifest presence in the Scripture include:

1. Moses and the burning bush (Exodus 3:1-10)

2. The pillar of fire and the pillar of cloud (Exodus 13:20-22)

3. The threshing floor of Araunah (2 Samuel 24:16-25)

4. Shiloh (1 Samuel 1:1-3; Joshua 18:1-2)

5. Mountain of transfiguration (Matthew 17:1-7)

Sometimes the manifest presence can be at a geographical location, which God has chosen to appear to His people and bless them.

Personalized Presence of God (Psalm 95:2)

This aspect of God's presence is what we call the requested and revealed presence of God that is available to God's people as they follow a biblical pattern of prayer, fasting, worship and seeking of God.

This personalized presence can be sought by all believers and can be granted, as we personally seek the Lord in consecration, devotion, praise, worship, prayers, and meditation on the Scripture.

This personalized presence of God is particularly made known to us individually and collectively as we seek Him (Psalm 103:7; 22:3; 51:11; 16:11; 31:20).

CONCLUSION

We must continually seek the presence of God. Revival is a time when the presence of God moves from the omnipresent manifest presence of God to the revealed personalized presence of God. Let us continue to pursue His presence and Satan will have no place around us or in us.

PRAYER

1. Oh Lord, reveal yourself in me.

2. Oh Lord, show me your glory; show me your presence and your power.

3. Oh Lord, let your presence break my mountain of problem into pieces.

4. Oh lord, let your presence be revealed in me, and let my mountains and hills be blown away like chaff.

NOTES

_____

_____

_____

_____

_____

_____

NOTES

_____

_____

_____

_____

_____

_____

_____

_____

_____

STUDY 5

ATTITUDES THAT QUENCH REVIVAL

TEXT: 1 THESSALONIANS 5:19-21

Apostle Paul exhorted the Thessalonian church to do the things that would allow for the continuance of the work of the Holy Spirit. Revival is nothing but the full manifestation of the presence and works of the Holy Spirit in us and among us. Wrong attitudes and dispositions can drive away the presence of the Holy Spirit and hinder the progress of revival. We can talk about revival, pray for revival, and wish for revival, but without the proper attitude towards revival and in a revival, revival cannot be seen or sustained.

The expression, "Do not quench the Spirit", means:

- Don't stop the flow of the Spirit.

- Don't put out the light of the Spirit.

- Don't extinguish the Spirit fire.

- Don't stifle the utterance of the Spirit.

Quenched Revival – the Shiloh Example

Jeremiah 7:1-4,10-14

Shiloh was an example of a church or community in revival. The revival in Shiloh was so great that there was no mountain, yoke or problem that could not be surmounted there. Note, for instance:

- At Shiloh, Hannah received the blessing of birthing the first major prophet, Samuel (1 Samuel 1:10-20)

- God appeared in Shiloh (1 Samuel 3:1-4).

- At Shiloh, God subdued enemies (Joshua18:1).

- At Shiloh, God divided and gave inheritance to His people (Joshua 18:10).

When you consider Shiloh, you will discover that it was a place of glory, power, honor, manifest presence of God and revival; yet, the same Shiloh was soon forsaken and abandoned by God (Jeremiah 7:10-14). Why?

1. The iniquities of the priests (1 Samuel 2:12-14)

The priests were the first culprit in the departure of God's presence from Shiloh. This was because of their greed, lust, fornication and injustice in the service of God.

2. The iniquities of the people (Jeremiah 7:3-10)

- The people oppressed strangers

- The people oppressed the fatherless

- They did not execute judgment; there was injustice.

- The people oppressed widows

- The people stole, and committed murder and adultery

All these iniquities drove away the presence of God from Shiloh. So, God is simply in Jeremiah 7:12-14, "If I can drive away my presence away from Shiloh, I can also cause any revival to either cease or not take place at all, if there is no proper attitude towards the Holy Spirit."

Therefore Paul urges the church in Thessalonica not to quench the Spirit, because they were in the midst of a revival (1 Thessalonians 5:15-21).

Indicators of Revival

What are the characteristics of a church in revival or on the verge of revival?

1. The church experiences a new power and passion for the proclamation and demonstration of the gospel (1 Thessalonians1:5-6).

2. The church continuously resists the infiltration of an idolatrous culture of a religious spirit (1 Thessalonians 1:9).

3. The church is not shaken by faith contradictions and every wind of doctrine (1 Thessalonians 3:1-3).

4. The church makes personal holiness a serious objective, especially sexual purity (1 Thessalonians 4:1-8).

5. The church encourages true spirituality in personal life, ministry and business (1 Thessalonians 4:9-12).

6. The church wisely follows a proven leadership (1 Thessalonians 5:12-13).

7. The church clearly pursues biblical wholeness for each individual in a defined biblical process (1 Thessalonians 5:23-24).

8. The church establishes sound doctrine as its foundation and not religious trends, emotional spiritual experiences or charismatic personalities (2 Thessalonians 1:5-12; 2:10-11).

9. The church guards against spiritual gullibility and the spirit of merchandise that exalts experiences above the objective truth of the New Testament. (2 Thessalonians 2:9-17).

Revival Quenchers (Galatians 5:16-26)

1. Strife (Proverbs 17:14, 19; 22:10). This grieves and drives the Holy Spirit away quickly

2. Sedition and schism (1 Corinthians 12:25). This has to do with deliberate discrimination, marginalization, racism and criticism in the church.

3. Resistance to new move of the Spirit – that is, resistance to change or the unfamiliar (Matthew 23:13)

4. Negative influence on people's lives, corrupting people by blasphemy (Matthew 23:15)

5. Excessive emphasis on formalism. Focusing on human traditions, rules and regulations that have no scriptural or divine backing (Matthew 23:16-22).

6. Focusing on materialism, monetary gain and spiritual profiteering (Matthew 23:23–24). This happens when there is too much emphasis on money, while neglecting the "weightier matters of the law".

7. Externalizing spirituality. (Matthew 23:25-28). Camouflaging with a form of godliness, while harboring all manner of godlessness within.

8. Spiritual emptiness (Matthew 23:28-40). Emphasizing on gifts rather than the fruit of righteousness.

9. Lip service without heart service (Matthew 15:8-9).

10. Worshiping the vessel, instead of the creator of the vessel (Matthew 23:29-30)

11. Insensitivity towards people's problems(M a t t h e w 23:4).

12. Disobedience to the Holy Spirit

13. Negligence of personal spiritual discipline (1 Peter 2:11)

14. Immorality (1 Thessalonians 4:1-4)

15. Rebellion against constituted authority (Romans 13:1-2)

16. Lack of understanding and knowledge of the word of God and the moves of God (1 Corinthians 15:34; 1 Thessalonians 4:5).

CONCLUSION

If we are to have the move of God and revival among us, we need to move from the elementary doctrines of Christ. Let us move from attitudes and dispositions that can quench the Spirit. Such include strife, gossiping, backbiting, pride, malice, lust, immorality, pursuit of our ways rather than the ways of God, as well as negligence of the word of God, true worship and soul winning.

PRAYER

1. Oh Lord, search me through and through and purge me from every attitude that can quench the Spirit.

2. Oh Lord, don't let me be a hindrance to your move because of my attitude; change me and transform me.

3. Holy Spirit, open my eyes to see you; let me see myself in the light of your word, and empower me to change.

NOTES

_____

_____

_____

_____

_____

_____

_____

NOTES

STUDY 6

THE KEY TO REVIVAL (TOUCHING HEAVEN IN PRAYER)

TEXT: EZEKIEL 22:30-31; JEREMIAH 9:1,17-19; ISAIAH 21:11-12; REVELATION 5:1-8

The scripture is noticeably clear about the place of prayer in the Kingdom of God. Prayer was practiced by every believing soul, from righteous Abel to John the revelator. It has been the vital breath of the church through the long centuries of her struggle on earth. Prayer, therefore, is a heavenly activity and a high calling that all believers are mandated to be engaged in. it is not just for selected few - pastors, apostles, prophets, evangelists or teachers; it is a vocation in which anyone who desires to succeed on earth in his or her pilgrim's journey towards heaven must be involve. Any successful life, business, governance and leadership must be rightly engaged and involved in this holy calling.

Leonard Ravenhill said of prayer, "Prayer is the work that we must do to see GOD move in the world." Jesus said it even better and more authoritatively, "**Men always ought to pray and not lose heart.**" (Luke 18:1)

What then is prayer?

Prayer is conversation and communion with God. It is the infusion of God's ability into man's inability; the coming together of man's nature with Gods nature to form God's supernatural in man. It is not just a form of contemplation or meditation but also a direct address to him (God). Therefore, prayer may be oral, mental, occasional or constant.

In essence, prayer is:

- Beseeching the Lord (Exodus 3:21)

- Pouring out of the soul before God (1 Samuel 1:15).

- The travailing of the soul (Isaiah 53:11-12)

- Crying to heaven   (2 Chronicles 32:20)

- Bowing the knees to God (Ephesians 3:14)

Biblical Examples of Praying Believers and the Results

- Abraham's servant prayed to God and God directed him to the person who should be the wife of his master's son (Genesis 24:10-20).

- Jacob prayed to God and God melted the heart of

his infuriated brother, such that they met in peace and friendship (Genesis 32:24-30).

- Samson prayed to God and God showed him a well where he quenched his burning thirst and so lived to judge Israel (Judges 15:18-20)

- David prayed and God defeated the coursed of Ahitophel (2 Samuel 15: 31; 16: 20–23, 17: 14 – 33).

- Daniel prayed and God enabled him both to tell the king his dream and to give the interpretation (Daniel 2:16-23).

- Esther and Mordecai prayed, and God defeated the purpose of Haman (Esther 4:15-17, 6:7-8).

- The believers in Jerusalem prayed, God opened the prison doors and set Peter at liberty (Acts 12:1-12).

The Power of Prayer

As Robinson Job said, "Prayer is like the dove that Noah sent forth, which blessed him not only when it returned with an olive-leaf in its mouth, but when it never returned at all"

Prayer is an effective means of communication with God; it gives us dominion over all that God has created. Prayer is the link between man and God. By it we perfume the heavens (Revelation 5:8). Indeed, without prayer, progress and growth will be a mirage in the church. This is why the apostles said in Acts 6:4, **"But we will give ourselves continually to prayer…"**

So, what happens when you pray?

1. It clears your head.

2. It clears your eyes.

3. It clears your mind.

4. It clears your heart.

5. It charges up your spirit.

6. It infuses the Spirit of heaven into your spirit.

7. It gives your spirit man confidence and makes you clean.

8. It releases heaven's aroma on you.

9. It sends demons away from you.

10. It perfumes the throne of heaven and gladdens the heart of God.

11. It makes your angel to continue to win battles (see Daniel's case in Daniel 10:10-20). It is the food that feeds your angel with strength and helps him to keep on fighting your battles.

12. It brightens your face and lightens your burdens (Psalm 3:4)

13. It empowers you with desire and craving for holiness and righteousness.

14. It births a fresh hunger for the word of God in you.

15. It causes the word of God to have meanings and revelations to you.

16. It makes heavenly powers available to you, especially when coupled with fasting.

17. It changes your perception of things, situations and people.

18. It causes satanic powers in operation to crash.

19. It releases heavenly covering and protection upon you.

20. It forces kings to bow and prostrate to you before God. (See the case of Nebuchadnezzar before Daniel in Daniel 2:46).

21. It makes all kinds of grace available to you.

CONCLUSION

Prayer is potent. It is efficacious, and when delivered through the engine of righteousness, holiness and purity with genuine fasting, it paralyzes the powers of darkness.

PRAYER

1. Oh Lord, teach me how to pray.

2. Holy Spirit, help me to pray according to your will and mind.

3. Father, restore my candle light of prayer and make me enjoy the communion of heaven, as you bring down your glory and power over my life.

NOTES

_____

_____

_____

_____

_____

_____

_____

NOTES

STUDY 7

THE KEY TO REVIVAL (2)
(The Ministry Of Intercession And Supplication)

TEXT: EZEKIEL 22:30-31; ISAIAH 2:11-12; LUKE 18:1-18; ACTS 12: 1-18

Having had some understanding of what prayer is in the previous study, we need to look further into the deeper dimensions of the prayer ministry, such as intercession and supplication. This is necessary because, contrary to what most of us Christians believe about prayer - especially that it is all about asking for personal things from God - prayer is much more than that

Prayer therefore is the turning of the soul towards God to seek nothing but God Himself (Psalm 25:1). When we lift our souls to God in prayer, it gives God the opportunity to do what He wills in us and with us. It also putting ourselves at God's disposal to use us in stopping the works of the enemy.

Therefore, one of the deeper dimensions of prayer beyond asking and receiving   personal requests is the prayer of intercession and supplication.

What is Intercession? (Ezekiel 22:30-31; Genesis 18:16-33)

The word intercession is from the Greek word *"enteusis"*, which means meeting with, petitioning, advocating, or soliciting on behalf of someone - just as a lawyer will do in a law court, as he pleads the case of his client before the judge to win approval, mercy or justice. The same word is translated as prayer in 1 Timothy 4:5 and 2:1.

In the Bible parlance, it is also the same word as "standing in the gap", which implies, standing as a middleman; an arbitrator between two parties, each demanding justice and equity.

Examples of intercessors in the Bible

1. Abraham interceded on behalf of Lot in the land of Sodom and Gomorrah (Genesis 18:16-30).

2. Esther interceded on behalf of the Jews in the land of Persia, seeking God's mercy, lest they should be destroyed (Esther 4:15-17;7:1-10).

3. Daniel interceded on behalf of the Jews in captivity in the land of Babylon. (Daniel 9:1-end).

4. The disciples interceded on behalf of Peter (Acts 12:1-8).

5. Paul the apostle interceded on behalf of the Ephesians, Galatians, Colossians, and all the churches in Asia (Ephesians 1:15-20).

6. Jesus interceded in the garden of Gethsemane (Luke 22:39-46).

7. Jesus still sit at the throne of the father, interceding for the saints (Hebrews 7:25; 12:1-3).

Why intercede?

- To avert danger and deception

- To cause restoration and renewal (Habakkuk 3:1-4)

- To receive mercy, favor, compassion, healing and health

- To obtain victory out of defeat

- Salvation and deliverance

- Growth and increase

- Stability and peace

- Fulfillment of promise

- Removal of obstacles and hindrances

- Breaking of demonic strongholds

For whom should we intercede? (I Timothy 2:1-4)

1. One another (Ezekiel 22:30)

Most Christians will not fall into sin and backslide or yield to discouragement and despondency, if fellow believers will remember to stand in the gap for one another. God said, I look for an intercessor, but I found none.

2. Our homes (Genesis 25:21; Lamentations 2:19)

Marriages are breaking down. Children are going wayward. Why? Because mothers have neglected the ministry of intercession and instead of having intercession spirit, they are possessed with the spirit of old wives' fables, fashion and worldliness. No wonder Satan is taking our husbands through adultery and our children by waywardness and the spirit of Belial.

Jeremiah cried, "...Teach your daughters wailing, And everyone her neighbor a lamentation" (Jeremiah 9:17-20).

3. The church (Isaiah 62:6-7)

If our church must grow, genuine, consistent and importunate intercession must be the cry of the church leaders and workers. Then will there be good health, growth, wealth, divine presence and conversion of souls.

4. Sinners (Galatians 4:19)

King David affirms that salvation belongs to God (Psalm 38:22). However, God cannot do much on earth without our intercession. if we are to see sinners come into our churches and get saved, we must cry out to

God, demanding for the harvest of souls. The prayer of Stephen in Acts 7:59-60 contributed to the eventual salvation of Paul, one of his killers.

What are the hindrances to prayer?

1. Unconfessed sin (Psalm 66:18)

2. Lack of faith (Hebrews 11:6; James 1:6-7)

3. Disobedience (1 John 3:21-23)

4. Unforgiveness (Matthew 6:14-15)

5. Wrong motives (James 4:2-4)

6. Disregard for others (Isaiah 58:4)

7. Unsurrendered will (John 15:7)

CONCLUSION

We must ask God for the pouring of the spirit of intercession and supplication upon us (Zechariah 12:10)

PRAYER

1. Oh Lord, give me grace to stand in the gap for my family, my community and my church.

2. Oh Lord, raise up among us, true intercessors, who will not seek their own interests but that which is of Christ and His body.

NOTES

NOTES

STUDY 8

STEPS TO GLORY AND THE ANOINTING

TEXT: MATTHEW 3:13-17; 2 KINGS 2:1-15,19-25; ISAIAH 61; PSALM 23; ACTS 10:38; ROMANS 15:17-19; 1 JOHN 2:27

You may wish to know what the "anointing" is and why you need it in your life. Is the anointing not only for the pastors, prophets, ministers of the gospels or church workers? NO! The anointing is for every believer.

The anointing is the manifest presence of God in a believer or upon a believer's life. It is the seal of approval of God's authority on a believer, as given by the Holy Spirit. It is given to believers in different measures.

When the appropriate steps of fellowshipping with God and seeking His presence and power are taken by the believer, the anointing, which is God's power for living a life of signs and wonders, is poured out on such.

Therefore, like King David, we must seek to be anointed with fresh oil and not in small measures. (Psalm 23:5; 92:10).

It is the desire of God to anoint us when we seek the anointing and take proper steps towards it. Mighty things will God wrought in our lives, families, businesses and ministries when we are anointed!

Isaiah 61:1-3 says, **"The Spirit of the Lord GOD is upon Me, Because the LORD has anointed Me To preach good tidings to the poor; He has sent Me to heal the brokenhearted, To proclaim liberty to the captives, And the opening of the prison to those who are bound; To proclaim the acceptable year of the LORD, And the day of vengeance of our God; To comfort all who mourn, To console those who mourn in Zion, To give them beauty for ashes, The oil of joy for mourning, The garment of praise for the spirit of heaviness; That they may be called trees of righteousness, The planting of the LORD, that He may be glorified."**

This shows that everyone is called into a particular business or endeavor, and that whatever you are called to do, you must be anointed to do it; for without the anointing of the Holy Spirit, there will be no glowing results - rather, it will be struggles and struggles alone.

Steps to the Anointing

Matthew 3:13-17; 4:1-6; 2 Kings 2:1-15

To fully comprehend the steps to the anointing, we will study the steps to the anointing in Jesus Christ life and the prophet Elisha. Their patterns will also give each of us the practical steps we must take to be properly anointed for our business, life, ministry, governance and leadership.

Understanding and following the steps that Jesus and Elisha took to be anointed provide a sure guarantee to the highest kind of anointing, power and glory that can be released upon you.

THE JESUS' STEPS TO THE ANOINTING

1. Go to your man of God or be connected to a higher anointing (Matthew 3:13).

Jesus left His place and went to John in Jordan. Jesus travelled from Galilee to meet John who was a senior priest, an anointed servant of God, who had the Spirit of God upon him that could break the heaven open upon Jesus (Luke 1:80; 3:1-2).

You must recognize and acknowledge the anointing on your man of God, pastor or prophet. Your connection and belief in that anointing also brings an anointing upon you.

2. Submit to your man of God

Matthew 3:13 says, "**Then Jesus came from Galilee to John at the Jordan to be baptized by him**"

Jesus recognized what God had place upon John - the grace, the unction, the anointing. Jesus went to John and submitted himself to him in baptism and as he did, the heavens over Him opened, the Spirit descended on Him and He was led by the Spirit to the wilderness for a higher anointing.

Put simply, if Jesus had not gone to John, the Spirit would not have descended upon Him.

3. Humble yourself in the Kingdom

"When all the people were baptized, it came to pass that Jesus also was baptized; and while He prayed, the heaven was opened" (Luke 3:21).

Despite the fact that Jesus knew that He was the Messiah, He never overrated himself. He humbled himself. He joined the people in the Kingdom to do what they were doing, which God had commanded through John.

Jesus' humility shows that it is only the humble that can be anointed.

4. Don't be led by men's opinion (Matthew 3:14)

Any man who wants to be anointed must avoid the mistake of being led by people's opinion. Even John the Baptist almost persuaded Jesus not to come to him, but Jesus understood that, to be anointed, it did not matter what John believed or felt; what mattered was that righteousness and the Scripture must be fulfilled.

5. Fulfill all righteousness – Matthew 3:14-16

To be anointed, you must obey constituted authorities and carry out spiritual injunctions and directives given by the senior man of God, under whom you serve.

6. Understand the timings of God

"But Jesus answered and said to him, Permit it to be so now" (Matthew 3:15).

The Kingdom of God operates with times and seasons. Jesus knew that to be anointed you must learn submission and obedience.

7. You must be obedient to God's voice (John 10:1-16)

Jesus was obedient to His Father. Whatever he heard His father speak was what he did. To be anointed and step into God's glory, we must hear his voice, know his word and do his word. The anointing comes in obedience.

8. Be prayerful (Luke 3:21)

We must pray for the anointing, we must pray for the Holy Spirit. Prayer is an important step to receiving the anointing. When we pray, the heavens rumble, and the Spirit is poured out upon us (Zechariah 10:1). When we pray, the heavens are opened and mighty strength and power are poured out upon us. (Matthew 3:16).

THE ELISHA'S STEPS TO THE ANOINTING (2 KINGS 2:1-15)

1. Be ready to serve God and your man of God (1 Kings 19:19-21).

Elisha became a servant and follower of Elijah in serving God. In the process, he had the special privilege to know when the man of God would be taken. This gave him the opportunity to be positioned for the anointing, due to his service.

Never run away from service. Never run away from your duty post. Your elevation in life, your anointing and your steps to spiritual progress and glory are in service.

2. Follow to Gilgal (2 Kings 2:1)

To be anointed, we must experience Gilgal in our lives as believers. Gilgal is a place of circumcision. (Joshua 5:2-10).

What is circumcision?

It is the removal of excess flesh and unwanted flesh that gives no beauty to our manliness in Christ. There is a physical circumcision, but spiritual circumcision is the removal of the flesh and its works (Galatians 5:19-21), which hinder the flow of God's Spirit and works in our lives.

To be anointed like Elisha, you must go with your man of God – that is, the leadership of the Holy Spirit, His teachings, His words and His instructions. All flesh must be cut off (Romans 2:26-29).

3. Follow to Bethel (2 Kings 2:2; Genesis 28:10-22)

Bethel, spiritually and symbolically, represents the house of God, the place of prayer! Jesus said, "**It is written, 'My house shall be called a house of prayer**" (Matthew 21:13). To be anointed, after Gilgal, symbolizing the removal of sinful flesh, one must enter into a lifestyle of fellowship, prayer, worship and devotion. These take you a step closer to the anointing and God's glory.

4. Follow to Jericho (2 Kings 2:4-5)

Jericho is place of warfare and intense of battle. It is the place of enemy's mockery which you must not give in to. The wicked will taunt you, but as you press on in warfare, God begins to appear to you as the Captain of the host of heaven. In other words, you begin to discover God anew. His miracles and His victories usher you into a new realm of glory and anointing; but, as already noted, this is not without intense warfare!

5. Follow to Jordan (2 Kings 2:6-15)

This is the realm of the Spirit. As you follow from the destruction of the flesh (Gilgal) to Bethel (the place of prayer), then to Jericho (the place of warfare) God leads you to the place of the outpouring of the Spirit; that is, the place of anointing and open heaven.

As Jesus was in Jordan being baptized and praying, the heaven was open for Him and the anointing descended.

CONCLUSION

The place of glory and anointing requires sacrifice, death of sin and flesh, as well as continuity in following God, until the heaven is opened for us, like Jesus by the Jordan River (Matthew 3:13-17).

PRAYER

Oh Lord, remove every work of the flesh from that is blocking your grace and anointing from manifesting in my life.

NOTES

_____

_____

_____

_____

_____

_____

_____

_____

_____

NOTES

STUDY 9

HONORING AND RESPECTING CONSTITUTED AUTHORITIES

TEXT: ROMANS 13:1-7; HEBREWS 13:7,17

Our attitude to constituted authorities, whether spiritual or governmental, will go a long way in determining the level of respect, honor and blessing we will receive. So, in this study, we will consider how God expects us as believers to relate to two kinds of authority:

1. Spiritual authority and

2. Government authority

Purpose of Authority (Judges17:6; Judges 19, 20; Malachi 2:7)

Imagine a nation without a leader, an organization without a boss, an army without a general. There will be lawlessness, disorder, confusion and lack of progress. Believers must pay their taxes, obey traffic laws, and vote during elections. In other words, we must give to Caesar what belongs to Caesar (Mark 12:14–17)

There are three fundamental purposes of leadership and authority (both spiritual and governmental).

1. To give direction

2. To create peace and order

3. To bring prosperity and progress

As 1 Timothy 2:1-3 makes us to understand, God has placed authorities over our lives, so that we may lead a good and peaceful life.

Measure of Your Spirituality (Romans 13:1-7)

"Render therefore to all their due: taxes to whom taxes are due, customs to whom customs, fear to whom fear, honor to whom honor" (Romans 13:7).

The degree to which you are submitted to the Lord is revealed in your attitude towards those whom God has placed in positions of authority over you. God works and speaks primarily through men and women. He honors offices of leadership. God speaks to us through human agents, such as husbands, wives, teachers, pastors, political office holders, community leaders and law enforcement agents. To ignore such authority is to ignore God's authority (I Thessalonians 4:8).

God Honors the Leader and His Office (1 Samuel 3:1-3)

Eli was a man of God, who at the time of his serving in the temple, things were not right. His eyes were dim, signifying spiritual partial blindness (1 Samuel 3:2-3); and the lamp in the temple was out. Yet, even in this spiritual condition, he was still the high priest in Israel, an exalted position that must not be looked down upon by man or God. As a proof of this, God, in his mercy, honored the position and words of Eli, when he prayed for Hannah (1 Samuel 1:8-20).

From the foregoing, the following lessons are noteworthy:

1. We must not despise spiritual authority no matter the spiritual condition or state of mind of the personalities involved. The one who has appointed them knows how to deal them. Complaining against God's servants instead of praying for them can cause "Taberah" - the fire of God's wrath (see Numbers 11:1-3).

2. Dishonoring God's servants or undermining their spiritual authority and office can cause spiritual leprosy, financial leprosy or family leprosy. One becomes a spiritual outcast. Grace, favor and mercy will depart from such (Numbers 12:1-13).

3. Dishonoring God's servants or undermining their spiritual authority can cause setbacks and delays, as

well as spiritual and physical retrogression to a whole congregation (Numbers 12:14-16).

4. Never speak against God's anointed! (See the examples of Korah, Dathan and Abiram in Numbers 16:1-35).

Called to Submission, not Sinfulness (Ephesians 5:21; 1 Peter 2:13-14, 18)

We are called to submission to all legally constituted authorities placed by God on us, as long as what they ask us to do is not out of God's will. We must obey their call to righteous living, praying with the right motives, godly meetings and holy convocations. An authority like Nebuchadnezzar that calls for the worship of an idol is part of the exceptions. We must not obey such (Daniel 3:8-30).

Except when their instructions violate God's words, whenever we rebel against constituted authorities, we are indirectly rebelling against God. As someone rightly said, "The person who says, 'I am just not going to listen to any man. I listen only to the Lord', is not listening to the Lord either." Why? Because the word of God says to obey them that have the rule over you (Hebrews 13:17).

Note the following:

• Churches, ministries, pastors, prophets, leaders, wives, children, husbands and citizens who do not submit to the instructions and directives of constituted authorities are in direct rebellion against Christ and His Spirit. Whoever does so is possessed by another spirit, which is the spirit of the antichrist; and there is only one solution if such persists in rebellion, which is to cast him out (Revelation 12:7-12).

- Anyone who despises authorities or disobeys their instructions is also operating by the spirit of Queen Vashti. Her sentence? Dethronement. (Esther 1:10-22).

- Disobeying and disrespecting authority is the same as dishonoring and despising the heavenly apparatus and authority that established God's anointing and leadership upon his servant. This God does not treat lightly (Esther 1:16-18).

CONCLUSION

Respect those in authority over you. Your success in life - spiritually, physically and financially - is affected by it. The Spirit of God is the Spirit of order, respect and liberty. Let us eliminate every rebellion against constituted authorities! Obey your general overseer and all the leaders that God has placed over you at all levels in the church and outside the church. It attracts divine favor and blessings.

PRAYER

1. Oh Lord, deal with every pride and rebellion in me against constituted authority.

2. Oh Lord, deliver me from the spirit of Lucifer and Queen Vashti that wants to disgrace me.

3. Help me, Lord, to have regard for all authorities you have constituted over me - my pastor, my husband, my boss and the government of the land.

4. Oh Lord, arrest every spirit of lawlessness in me, in Jesus' name.

5. Oh Lord, kill every marine spirit in me, and the spirit of the assembly of Korah, Dathan and Abiram that wants to destroy my glorious destiny in Christ.

NOTES

NOTES

STUDY 10

A CHURCH WITH A DIFFERENCE
(Non-Conformity to the World)

TEXT: ROMANS 12:2; 1 JOHN 2:15-17

As believers in Christ, we are not forbidden from benefitting from the usefulness of the liberal arts, important discoveries, scientific innovations and the technologies of the modern world. Christians are not only privileged but also bound to avail ourselves of gadgets and inventions that make life easier. We must maximize them for our personal lives and the advancement of God's work.

However, we have been strictly warned not to conform to the world (adopt the worldly way of thinking and living) in the following areas: Business, fashion and politics. In these areas, Christians should not do as the people of the world do or adopt their principles. We must not act from the same motives or pursue objectives in the same manner the world does.

Why non-conformity in business? (1 John 2:15-17)

1. The principle of this world in business is selfishness (Proverbs 11:1). This is not the Spirit of Christ.

2. The system of this world is destruction of others to their advantage (John 10:10). The worldly people steal, kill and use other people to achieve their own ambition. Christ came to give life and seek others' wellbeing.

3. The worldly pattern of business is ruled by cheating, looting and selfishness, with no regards for God's commands or the welfare of their fellow men. (Proverbs 13:11-13).

4. The businessmen of this world are primarily concerned about their own interests, even if it is at the expense of the people they relate with. The word of God to us is clear, however, as believers - there should be non-conformity to the world. We must seek the interest and wellbeing of others (1Corinthians 10:24).

5. Conformity to the world in business practices is inconsistent with the love of God (Leviticus 19:35-37)

Biblical Business Principles

*   Seek the interest of others first (Philippians 2:4). When you make men see what is in it for them first,

they are happy and delighted to want to do business with you.

- Avoid deception
- Avoid cut-throat gain that is detrimental to others
- Let Christ drive your conscience

Non-conformity in fashion (Jeremiah 10:1-2; 1 Peter 3:3-6). Believers must not conform to the pattern of this world in fashion. Our dressing must be modest and that which reveals and honors Christ in our life (1 Timothy 2:9-10). Any dressing that does not cover the body or exposes the sensitive parts or causes sexual lusts in others is not of Christ; it is of the world and must be done away with. Your dressing reveals who you are and what is in you. The way you dress will determine the way men will address you. God looks into the heart but men judge by your outlook, not your inward.

Consider the case of Moses in Exodus 2:11-20.

Was Moses an Egyptians or an Israelite? Yes! Moses was an Israelite by birth. However, Moses had lived with Egyptians. Moses dressed like an Egyptian. And so Moses was addressed as an Egyptian though he was an Israelite!

Many believers are like Moses – they are born-again. But, sadly, because they are living and working among unbelievers, they have allowed their dressing to also be like those of unbelievers!

We are commanded to be different and separate from the world in our talks, mannerisms, way of life and fashion (1 Corinthians 6:11-17). In verse 17, we are critically commanded, "Come out from among them and be separate!

Dare to be different (1 Samuel 8:4-6)

God wants us to be different in our dressing. We must not be like other nations. As believers, though we are in this world, we are not of the nations of this world. Our citizenship is of heaven and we must dress and do like the people who are heaven-bound! (John 17:16; Ephesians 2:19)

The attire of the harlot (Proverbs 7:6-21)

The world of fashion is directly at war with the Spirit of the Gospel. Indeed, worldliness is best detected in people who zealously follow the fashions of the world that continually fluctuates in their forms!

Solomon described the woman in the above passage as having the attire of a harlot. There are many attires of a harlot today in the name of fashion which have also entered the church. It is so worrisome that sometimes, one cannot differentiate between a harlot and a normal decent woman or man.

Let us examine ourselves. The harlot dresses to kill - to kill his or her prey who is a precious soul to God and his family (Proverbs 6:26). This should not be our thinking or motive too, as believers.

Characteristics of the harlot's dressing

The harlot dresses to:

1. Expose sensual parts of the body

2. Attract the opposite sex

3. Kill the opposite sex

4. Seduce the opposite sex, though he or she tells you that is not the reason. "I dress to feel good" is what they say. But inwardly, they are hunters.

5. Cause distractions in an office, occasion, or congregation.

6. Reveal body parts that can ensnare the gullible and careless.

7. Seduce unwatchful men.

Non-conformity in Politics

Christians must be distinct. We are called to be God's own people.

Therefore, our own way of politics must be different from that of the people of this world. The politics of this world is entirely dishonest.

We must ensure we do not vote into power men whom we know do not fear God or favor His cause!

CONCLUSION

The Scripture warns us in 1 John 2:15-17, never to love the world or the things in the world, for the love of the world is enmity with God (James 4:4). All that is in the world is lust of the flesh (immorality), lust of the eyes (covetousness) and pride of life. These are not of God.

We must live differently from unbelievers. The world must see the difference in us and through us. We are pacesetters. We must be non-conformists to the ways of the world, but rather conformists to the way of the Lord.

PRAYER

1. Oh Lord, grant me the grace and strength to be different.

2. Oh Lord, destroy every lust for the things of the world in me in Jesus' name.

NOTES

NOTES

_____

_____

_____

_____

_____

_____

_____

_____

_____

STUDY 11

STEPS TO VICTORY OVER SIN IN CHRIST

TEXT: ROMANS 8:1 – 15

Reginald Wallis once said, "The triumphant Christian does not fight for victory, he celebrates a victory already won." Many believers desire victory over sin and they constantly wonder why sin seems to have a grip on them, even when the scriptures says sin shall have no dominion over them (Romans 6:14).

The question is, if God's law forbids certain practices, why can't we just obey God and stop doing what he forbids? The truth is that telling people that what they are doing is wrong does not give them power to stop doing wrong.

In fact, the power of sin is aroused by the existence the law and the Adamic nature within us (Romans 7:5). So, instead of the law helping to stop sin, it actually stimulates what it is meant to prohibit. This is natural as "the forbidden fruit always appears desirable." Proverbs 9:17 affirms that stolen waters always appears to be sweeter.

So, how do we overcome sin?

SECRETS OF VICTORY OVER SIN

1. Your identity in Christ (Galatians 2:19-20; 3:19-29; 5:1 – 16)

Before we come to Christ, we are dead in sins and walk in our lusts and the passions of this world. But the moment we receive Christ, we are made dead to the world and alive to God (Galatians 2:20; Ephesians 2:1-3).

At salvation, a change takes place and a new power is induced in the believer to live victoriously in Christ (Ephesians 5:8; Romans 8: 8-9).

Therefore, your victory in Christ starts with your identification in Christ.

For believers to be victorious in Christ, the sin-consciousness must be broken and the Christ-consciousness must be awakened.

You must walk in the light of who you are in Christ Jesus – this is the first basic step to your victory in Christ over sin.

2. Realize who you are

In Christ, you are:

- A new creature (2 Corinthians 5:17)

- God's child (John 1:12)

- Jesus' friend (John 15:15)

- Holy and accepted by God (Romans 5:1)

- United with the Lord and one in spirit with Him (1 Corinthians 6:17)

- Bought with a price, and therefore God's property (1 Corinthians 6:20)

- A member of God's family (1 Corinthians 12:27)

- A saint (Ephesians 1:1)

- Adopted and have direct access to God (Ephesians 1:5; 2:18)

- Complete in Christ (Colossians 2:10)

3. You are dead to sin (Romans 6:1 – 14)

- The laws of God and the ways of God do not operate in the same way with the laws of the natural world.

- The word of God says we are dead to sin and that is what it is.

- We don't feel dead, but we are dead to sin.

- We must walk in the consciousness of what Christ has done, nailing sin to the cross and making us alive to Himself.

You must believe the word of God, even if your feeling doesn't match what it says. It is not the same as denying your emotion, but rather it is agreeing with God.

(4)   Alive in Christ (Romans 6:4-5)

The moment we accepted Jesus Christ as our Lord, we not only died with Him, but we were also made alive with Him. So, we are spiritually alive to God in Christ and dead to sin in Him.

So as children of God "In Christ", we identify with Him in the following ways:

- In His death   -   Romans 6:3,6;
                                   Galatians 2:20,
                                   Colossians 3:1-3

- In His burial   -   Romans 6:4

- In His resurrection   -   Romans 6:5, 8,11

- In His ascension   -   Ephesians 1:19-20

- In His inheritance   -   Romans 8:16-17

CONCLUSION

To have victory over sin, you must reckon your body as dead to sin, declare the finished works of Christ in your life and walk in His power, freedom and liberty. Galatians 5: 1.

Move unto practical Christian living and victorious Christian living by not yielding to your flesh. (Romans 8:2-10)

PRAYER

1. I declare that the blood of Jesus has set me free.

2. I declare that, by his Spirit, I have dominion over sin.

3. I live above the flesh through the Spirit of grace.

NOTES

_____

_____

_____

_____

_____

_____

NOTES

STUDY 12

BREAKING THE SIN CONSCIOUSNESS

TEXT: 2 CORINTHIANS 5:17 – 21

One of the greatest challenges a believer faces as to walking in the righteousness of God is breaking free from sin consciousness. Therefore, we need to consider practical ways to abandon sin consciousness and increase our righteousness consciousness.

The Reality (2 Corinthians 5:21; Romans 5:17 -19)

Once we are born again, we are a new creation - this implies a being that never existed before. We have been reconciled to God and have become His ambassadors to the world. But, more importantly, we have become the "righteousness of God" in Jesus Christ.

Sin entered the world by one man, and by one man righteousness entered the world. (Romans 5:17-19). The gift of righteousness was given to as many who have received Christ. The power to walk in righteousness and be righteous is given to us by Christ(John 1:12; 17:20-23). Therefore, our righteousness is impacted by Christ and we should move to a greater level and confidence in righteousness (Romans 4:17).

Jesus is made the righteousness of God for our benefit. God also made Him wisdom, redemption and sanctification for our benefit. Therefore, we must receive Christ as the only way by which we can be righteous always (1 Corinthians 1:30).

The Sin Nature and the Sin Consciousness (Romans 7:7-25)

- Sin is a nature inherited and inherent in man from birth (Psalm 51:5)

- The sin nature is in all men (Romans 3:23)

- Sin came in by one man (Romans 5:17-19)

- Jesus destroyed the sin nature (1 John 3:8).

- It is only by faith in Christ Jesus finished work on the cross that we can be saved from sin (Galatians 3:11-13; Ephesians 2:1-15).

Practical Steps to Breaking the Sin Consciousness

1. Meditate upon the word of God (Joshua 1:8)

2. Think upon your inheritance and who you are in Christ

3. Never walk in the company of sinners (Psalm 1:1-3)

4. Forsake the assembly of mockers and the wicked (Jeremiah 15:17)

5. Eat the word of God raw and do it (Jeremiah 15:16)

6. Maintain good works and good deeds of righteousness (Titus 3:3-14)

7. Learn to deny ungodliness; don't feed on the things of the flesh. (For example, movies that spark up lust and talks that encourage iniquity - avoid them). (Titus 2:11-12).

8. Never be unequally yoked with unbelievers. (2 Corinthians 6:17-18; 2 Peter 2:20-21).

9. Don't play or joke with sin. Sin is like a snake, if you play with it, it will bite you and it will kill you. So, kill it before it kills you (Hebrews 10:26-29)

10. Be filled with the Spirit (Galatians 5:16)

CONCLUSION

Realize you do not have a license to sin; you have a license to practice the righteousness of God.

PRAYER

1. I break every mentality of sin consciousness in me, in Jesus' name.

2. I declare I am free from the law of sin and death.

3. I claim my victory in Christ Jesus.

4. I declare I am the righteousness of God in Christ Jesus.

5. I receive strength and grace to walk in righteousness always.

NOTES

_____

_____

_____

_____

_____

_____

_____

_____

NOTES

THE OPERATION OF MERCY IN A BELIEVER'S LIFE

TEXT: HEBREWS 4:15-16

It is one thing for you to know that God is merciful; it is another thing for you to have an understanding of how that mercy will operate in your life in practical ways as a believer. The focus of this teaching is to help us understand and appreciate the mercy of God in our lives, spiritually, physically, emotionally and financially.

Where we were before now (Ephesians 2:1-3)

According to the scripture above, we were dead in sin, cut off from the life and the light of God; but through the love of Christ and the mercy of God, we were brought back to God's light. Before now:

- We were enemies of God (Colossians 1:21)

- We were dead in sin (Ephesians 2:1)

- We were foreigners to God (Ephesians 2:12)

- We were excluded from the covenant of promise. (Ephesians 2:12)

- We were without hope (Ephesians 2:12)

But now in Christ Jesus we have received:

- Mercy

- Grace

- Truth

- Salvation

- Redemption

We were quickened by God in Christ Jesus, because He is RICH IN MERCY.

Conviction vs Condemnation

(Romans 8:1-4; Galatians 4:1; John 16:5-10)

- Part of the work of mercy of God is to bring us conviction and not condemnation.

- Often, a believer who has sinned will mistake conviction for condemnation. When you blow it, two things usually happen: the Spirit of God moves in to convict you of that sin. This is an act of mercy by the Holy Spirit (1 John2:1-2); secondly, the devil moves in to condemn you.

- Note that conviction is designed by God to bring you back to Himself, the source of life. (John 16:8-10); while condemnation is designed by the devil to shame you and pull you away from God. Satan wants to drive a wedge between you and God. (1 John1:9; Romans 8:1).

Take Hold Of The Mercy Of God (Hebrews 4:15-16)

We need the mercy of God but how do we get it?

We must come before His throne with humility and genuine repentance.

Benefits of Mercy

1. Mercy will heal you (Psalm 6:2)

2. Mercy will lift you from the gate of death (Psalm 9:13)

3. Mercy will bring you deliverances (Psalm18:50)

4. Mercy will bring you joy and gladness (Psalm 3:7)

5. Mercy will bring correction (Job 37:13).

6. Mercy will make men to favor you (Nehemiah 1:11)

7. Mercy will bring you out of any bondage - spiritual, physical or financial. (Ezekiel 9:9).

CONCLUSION

Mercy will cause a new flow of grace, restoration and anointing upon your life. It is time to cry for mercy like blind Bartimaeus again.

PRAYER

1. Oh Lord, have mercy upon me.

2. Father, Lord, in Jesus name, cause your mercy to save me, deliver me, purge me and sanctify me.

3. Lord, let mercy speak for me, before the throne of heaven, and before men and let my favor come.

NOTES

NOTES

STUDY 14

THE HEART OF MAN

TEXT: ROMANS 10:10; MARK 11:23; MATTHEW 15:18-21; JEREMIAH 17:9

The word "heart" here does not refer to the physical organ in man that pumps blood around his body; rather, it refers to the spiritual part of man, which controls his thoughts and directs his life.

The heart of man is his very core - the very center of his being, which governs his life and predetermines his actions, beliefs and practices. This is why Proverbs 4:27 counsels, "Keep your heart with all diligence,

For out of it spring the issues of life." This means that in our Christian walk, life endeavors and belief patterns (towards God, business, marriage, church and other areas of life), our heart plays an important role.

Therefore, in this study, we shall consider how our heart affects our life and our eternity.

Man is a Spirit (1 Thessalonians 5:23)

The term "spirit of man" and "heart of man" are used interchangeably throughout the Bible. So, God is Spirit (John 4:24); and man is also a spirit, because he was made in the image and likeness of God.

For a man to relate to God, he must relate to Him from his heart, that is, his spirit. A believer is not one who says he is one with his mouth but one who believes in his heart and in his spirit (Romans 2:28-29).

He that is born of the flesh is flesh and he that is born of the Spirit (heart) of God is spirit (John 3:6). Every man has a spirit (heart), a soul and also lives in a body. Therefore, it is important that you keep your heart.

Functions of the Believer's Heart

1. With the heart, you believe (Romans 10:10).

2. Our heart is indwelt by the Holy Spirit (2 Corinthians 1:22).

3. We make holy melodies to God through our heart (Ephesians 5:19).

4. We obey and serve from the heart (Colossians 3:22).

5. Our souls are purified by the Holy Ghost through our heart (1 Peter 1:22).

6. The Holy Spirit confirms things to our spirit (heart) (Romans 8:16; 1 John 5:6).

7. We are sealed by the Holy Spirit and we receive this confirmation through the earnestness of the Holy Spirit in our heart (2 Corinthians 1:22).

Pollutants of the Heart (Proverbs 4:23)

The heart can be attacked and polluted by various ungodly invaders, which do not allow for the free flow of the Spirit. Such pollutants include:

1. Bitterness – (Hebrews 12:15; Job 7:11; Ephesians 4:31)

2. Evil imaginations (Genesis 6:5; Genesis 8:21)

3. Wicked thoughts (Deuteronomy 15:9)

4. Unprepared or Sanctified heart (2 Chronicles 12:14)

5. Evil Inclinations (Psalm 141:4)

6. Deceit (Proverbs 12:20)

7. Sorrow in the heart (Ecclesiastes 11:10)

CONCLUSION

Let us examine our heart constantly and find out if the things we allow in there can make for the flow of the Holy Spirit. Further, let us search ourselves and ask: If God should allow others to see the contents of our heart, what would they think of us? Anything that is not in accordance with Christ must never stay in our heart.

PRAYER

1. Oh Lord, purge my heart, through and through, by your Holy Spirit.

2. Search me, oh Lord, and remove every wickedness and thought from my heart.

3. Oh Lord, grant me grace to fill my heart with good things always.

4. Lord, let your Holy Spirit and your word fill my heart always.

5. Father, speak to my heart always and through my heart.

NOTES

_____

_____

_____

_____

_____

_____

_____

_____

_____

NOTES

Study 15

THE HOLY SPIRIT: HIS PERSON, WORKS AND ATTRIBUTES

Text: John 16:5-15; 1 John 5:7-8

The Holy Spirit is the third person of the Godhead called the Trinity. The Holy Spirit is a person, just like Jesus Christ. He has a personality. He can talk, see, hear, feel, laugh, love and be angry. The Holy Spirit is not just a force or a power surge; He is a being that operates as God Himself, for He Himself is God.

Though there are impersonal metaphors used to describe the Holy Spirit, such as fire, wind, water, oil, dove and so forth, all these are merely for describing some of His ways and attributes. In reality, the Holy Spirit is more than all of these; for He is God Himself.

The Holy Spirit as God

The Bible clearly calls the Holy Spirit God. For instance:

*   In Matthew 28:19, Jesus refers to the Holy Spirit in the order of God Himself.

- In Acts 5:3-4, Peter asks Ananias why he chose to lie to the Holy Ghost.

So, He is not just a force.

Moreover, the Holy Spirit does works that no other person can do, except God.

- The Holy Spirit created the heaven and earth - Genesis 1:2; Job 26:13

- He raised the dead – Romans 1:4

- He gives a new life for the New Birth – John 3:5-7

- He convicts the world of sin and judgment – John 16:7-8

- He casts out devils – Matthew 12:28

Attributes of the Holy Spirit

The Holy Spirit has the same attributes as God. These include being eternal, omnipotent, omnipresent and omniscient. As the scriptures reveal:

- Hebrews 9:14 - The Holy Spirit is eternal

- 1 Corinthians 2:10   – The Holy Spirit knows all things

- Luke 1:35 – The Holy Spirit is omnipotent

- Psalm 139:7– 8 - The Holy Spirit is omnipresent

The Holy Spirit Has a Personality

Until we begin to see the Holy Spirit as an entity who has a personality as do the Father and the Son, our posture towards the Holy Spirit will never change. When we see the Holy Spirit as a person like Jesus Christ with complete personality traits, then and then can our lives change and our walk with Him is endued with power.

The personality traits of the Holy Spirit

1. The Holy Spirit speaks – Revelation 2:7

2. The Holy Spirit helps us in our weakness – Romans 8:26

3. The Holy Spirit prays for us - Romans 8:26

4. The Holy Spirit teaches us - John 14:26

5. The Holy Spirit testifies to the Lord – John 15:26

6. The Holy Spirit guides us - John 16:13

7. The Holy Spirit commands people in their service – Acts 16:6-7

8. The Holy Spirit calls and anoints people for the work of God - Acts 13:2

9. The Holy Spirit comforts - Acts 9:31

10. The Holy Spirit has knowledge – 1 Corinthians 2:10; Romans 8:27

11. The Holy Spirit has emotions and feelings – Romans 5:5, Ephesians 4:30

12. The Holy Spirit has a will - 1 Corinthians 12:11; Act 16:6-7

Names of the Holy Spirit

The scripture uses, at least, four significant names to describe the Holy Spirit (also sometimes translated as the Holy Ghost). Such names include:

- The Spirit of Holiness or the Holy Spirit - 1 Thessalonians 4:7-8

- The Spirit of God – Ephesians 4:30; Genesis 1:2; 1 Corinthians 2:11; John 6:44;

- Matthew 11:25; Romans 8:11

- The Spirit of Christ - Romans 8:9; Acts 2:33

- The Comforter - John 15:26

- The Advocate (Paraclete) - John 14:16

When Jesus spoke of the Holy Spirit as another Comforter – He used the word "allos parakletos" – which means "the same kind of another comforter" or "another kind of comforter of the same person". This means that the Holy Spirit has the same personality, traits and attributes like Jesus. Whatever Jesus did while He was on earth, the Holy Spirit will do same for and through us.

Symbols of the Holy Spirit

The Holy Spirit is represented with various symbols. These symbols are to give us an understanding into His workings.

1. Water (John 7:37-38)

- The Holy Spirit quenches thirst for sin, and satisfies with heavenly life.

- He gives life. Though continuous drinking of the Holy Spirit, the water of life, our lives are preserved (1 Corinthians 12:13; John 4:13 -14).

- Water cleanses – (Titus 3:5)

2. Fire - Matthew 3:11

- God's presence often manifested as fire in the Old Testament

- God appeared to Moses in the burning bush of fire Exodus 3:1-5

- God came down in fire form when Elijah called on Him – 1 Kings 18

- On the day of Pentecost the Holy Ghost came down as cloven tongues of fire upon the believers. (Act 2:2-3)

- Fire burns the unwanted, which is a perfect method of purification (Hebrews 12:29, Jeremiah 23:29).

- Fire produce light

- Fire gives us supernatural zeal.

3. Wind (John 3:8, John 14:18)

The Greek word for wind and spirit is "pneuma'" while it is called "ruach" in Hebrew.

- The Holy Spirit is the Holy wind

- The wind is air in continuous motion. The Holy Spirit indwelling and infilling keeps us in continuous motion.

- The Holy Spirit flows into the area of low atmospheric pressure – sin, sickness, sorrow and despair and is ever ready to work in us given us the joyful message of forgiveness, healing and eternal life.

4. Oil (1Samuel 16:13; 1John 2 v 27)

- The oil is used to set apart people for God's work – Exodus 30:25-29; 3:30; 1 Kings 19:16.

- Oil is use to light candlesticks. The Holy Spirit lightens our candlesticks which is our spirit man. Zechariah 4:2- 6

- Oil prevents wear and tear and breakdown.

-

5. Rain - Psalm 72:6, Hosea 6:3, James 5: 7

- Rain helps us to bear fruits by watering our spiritual grounds

- The rain is the water that waters the seed of the gospel

- The rain typifies the outgoing nature of the spirit

6. Dove - John 1:32

- Dove is an emblem of peace

- It's a sign that we have passed from condemnation to peace (John 5:24, Rom 5 v1)

- The dove is a symbol of meekness and humility

- The dove is pure and harmless (Luke 4:18 -19)

- The dove is not easily grieved Eph. 4:30

7. Wine (Ephesians 5:18, Acts 2:12-13)

- Like wine, the Holy Spirit gladdens the heart of his drinkers – Psalm 104:15 While physical wine can dissipate energy and cause some harm, the wine of the Holy Spirit brings joy, life and strength. (Ephesians 5:19-21).

8. Seal (Ephesians 1:13)

- Seal means stamp. The Holy Spirit is the stamp of God upon our lives.
- It signifies of ownership
- It signifies authority

9. Guarantee (Corinthians 1:21 -22

The Holy Spirit is the symbol that we belong to God and we have great potentials, since the Lord is our manufacturer. He has the power and right to repair us, whenever we go wrong.

CONCLUSION

The Holy Spirit is the sweetest person on earth. Make Him your friend now, as knowing Him will be a great blessing to you. Relating with Him will be an experience that will usher you into unlimited glory.

We must develop a communication relationship with the Holy Spirit like we do with our fellow man – lover or spouse.

PRAYER

- Oh Lord, pour out your Spirit upon me
- Holy Spirit, fill me and reveal Christ in me and through me.
- Holy Spirit, take me to the next level of fellowship with you.

NOTES

NOTES

_____

_____

_____

_____

_____

_____

_____

_____

_____

www.ingramcontent.com/pod-product-compliance
Lightning Source LLC
Chambersburg PA
CBHW060946040426
42445CB00011B/1031